AF080797

AZHAR AL-RUBAIE

In the Shadow, in the Light
Interviews with the Iraqi LGBTQ+ Community

DRACOPIS PRESS

www.dracopis.com

beard@dracopis.com

Dracopis_012
Azhar Al-Rubaie
In the Shadow, in the Light; Interviews with the Iraqi LGBTQ+ Community
ISBN 978-91-87341-21-2 (SOFTCOVER)

© Azhar Al-Rubaie, 2025
Cover photo: © Sebastian Backhaus
Printed by Ingram, Worldwide
Published by Dracopis Press, Malmö, Sweden, 2025
Dracopis Press is an imprint of Smockadoll förlag
All rights reserved

Published with the support of
The Swedish Arts Council

9
Preface

11
Homosexuality in Iraq

21
Interviews

Sarah, 28, Baghdad
Boha, 27, Baghdad
Abdullah, 33, Baghdad
Laith, 25, Babylon
Hayden, 22, Najaf
Hussein, 26, Basra
Bash Taha, 34, Berlin
Azad Issa, 37, London

71
About the author

To those searching for love in troubled times,
To those who live with fear and uncertainty,
To those who hide their emotions out of fear of rejection,
To those who dream of peace and safety.
This book is for you,
To know that you are not alone,
That others feel the same way,
That there is hope for a better future.
This book is for you,
To stand up against injustice,
To fight for your right to love,
To help build a more just and compassionate society.
In both light and darkness, there are stories of forbidden love.
With sincere wishes for a life filled with love and happiness,
May darkness give way to light.

Preface

Nights and days, countless cups of coffee I have consumed. It took me a long time to come up with the title for my first book, *In the Shadow, in the Light*. This book tells the stories of individuals living in the shadows, and others whose lives were illuminated by light after a period of darkness. In the midst of darkness and light, love dances a silent dance. I delve into the tales of Iraqi LGBTQ+ individuals who have experienced both the shadows and the light. Within the pages of this book, you'll discover that love is forbidden for the LGBTQ+ community, while others bask in its warmth and affection.

The challenges and difficulties faced by members of the LGBTQ+ community are not limited to them alone, but extend to me as the author of this book. As a humbly well-known reporter, I have been able to leverage my reputation to build trust with individuals within the LGBTQ+ community, many of whom were initially hesitant to share their stories.

In this book, the echoes of shadow and light reverberate. Through the experiences of Iraqis, we embark on a journey together, exploring their stories of love, joy, hardship, suffering, fear, persecution, threats, and the unknown. These stories are woven into words written beyond the red lines, narrating what lies between, beneath, and far beyond those lines.

In the shadows, members of the LGBTQ+ community live in fear of societal norms and traditions that have forced them into secret lives. They fear rejection, marginalisation, and even violence. They also feel ashamed to express their feelings and emotions, searching for a glimmer of hope that might rescue them from their miserable existence and lead them to the light they have never tasted.

Others live under the sun of freedom in countries they were not born in, but sought out and found as a safe haven. They were able to find what they were denied in their homeland, Iraq: freedom, safety, and acceptance by society.

Through true stories from various cities across Iraq, members of the LGBTQ+ community, who most of them hide their identities in fear of imminent death, share their world of struggle, identity search, and freedom.

This enigmatic reality unveils profound human suffering, inspiring us all to stand against injustice, defend rights, and break taboos in the society that is angry at them. These individuals, who have sought and continue to seek justice and tolerance, have their own stories to tell. I also document the stories of those who were fortunate enough to escape seeking for safe and better life in the light. All of them have their stories waiting to be heard, and so the book *In the Shadow, in the Light* was written to narrate them. To protect the safety of the individuals involved, the names of most LGBTQ+ persons interviewed for this book have been changed.

I believe this book serves as a valuable resource for all readers and knowledge seekers, as well as those eager to hear the stories of LGBTQ+ individuals that they have not found in daily newspapers or online outlets. This is why this book holds such significance.

Homosexuality in Iraq

In ancient Mesopotamia (present-day Iraq), researchers believe that the renowned *Epic of Gilgamesh*, one of the world's oldest literary works, may hint at a homosexual relationship between its protagonists, Gilgamesh and Enkidu. While the epic does not explicitly state this, the intimate bond and shared adventures between the two heroes have led scholars to speculate about the nature of their relationship.

Although fictional, the *Epic of Gilgamesh* reflects aspects of Mesopotamian society and culture. The presence of themes related to homosexuality in this ancient text suggests that such themes were not entirely unknown or taboo in that era.

It's important to note that while the Epic of Gilgamesh provides intriguing clues, there is limited archaeological or textual evidence specifically addressing homosexuality in ancient Mesopotamia. Interpretations of ancient texts can vary depending on cultural and historical context.

Islam has traditionally held a negative view of homosexuality, rooted in interpretations of the Quran and Islamic law. This perspective often considers homosexual acts as deviant and harmful to society. However, historical accounts from the Safavid period in Mesopotamia suggest that there were instances of more tolerant attitudes towards sexual expression, with the legalisation of male brothels and the imposition of taxes on such establishments.

Following the U.S. invasion of Iraq in 2003 and the subsequent rise of Iran-backed militias, many LGBTQ+ Iraqis faced increased persecution and violence. These armed groups often targeted LGBTQ+ individuals, viewing them as deviants and threats to traditional Iraqi society. This violence included physical attacks, harassment, and even killings.

The situation for LGBTQ+ individuals in Iraq remains challenging, despite some progress in recent years. Discrimination and violence continue to be significant issues, and many LGBTQ+ Iraqis face the difficult choice of living in hiding or fleeing the country.

In 2010, a particularly gruesome campaign of violence unfolded, known as the 'Emo Murders.' This brutal series of killings specifically targeted young men perceived to be gay or to have non-traditional appearances. The victims were often tortured, mutilated, and killed in gruesome ways.

The perpetrators of these crimes were a mix of armed groups, including those affiliated with the Mahdi Army, a militia associated with the influential cleric Muqtada Al-Sadr. The attacks were driven by a toxic blend of homophobia and a desire to enforce rigid social norms.

The term 'emo,' derived from the word 'emotional,' emerged in the 1980s as a descriptor for a distinct subculture. Emo culture is characterised by a unique blend of music, fashion, and behaviour.

In the wake of the 'Emo Murders,' the Shiite leader Muqtada Al-Sadr further inflamed tensions by publicly condemning emo youths as 'crazy and a scourge of society.' He urged the legal authorities to take action against them, contributing to a climate of fear and intolerance.

Armed groups in Baghdad and other Iraqi cities followed Al-Sadr's lead, engaging in a campaign of brutal violence against the emo community. These attacks included horrific acts of torture, such as gluing victims' hair and anuses and forcing them to ingest laxatives. In some cases, the violence escalated to murder, with victims being stoned to death.

Since the US occupation of Iraq in 2003, armed groups in Iraq have carried out numerous acts of violence and persecution against the LGBTQ+ community, including kidnapping, rape, torture, and murder. These atrocities have been perpetrated with impunity, as security and judicial authorities have failed to hold perpetrators accountable.

The situation for the LGBTQ+ community in Iraq, particularly in the southern regions, is extremely dangerous. These areas are characterised by strict religious and cultural conservatism, tribal honour codes, and a lack of legal protection for LGBTQ+ individuals. The recent passage of Iraq's 2024 anti-LGBTQ+ law has further criminalised same-sex relationships and gender expression, exacerbating the risks faced by LGBTQ+ people.

Religious and cultural institutions often play a significant role in reinforcing discriminatory attitudes and practices. Transgender individuals and those in rural areas face unique challenges within the LGBTQ+ community. Despite these obstacles, activists, organisations, and international bodies are working to promote LGBTQ+ rights in Iraq.

LGBTQ+ individuals in Iraq face significant challenges within their families. Iraqi society's conservative views on sexual orientation and gender identity, combined with the strong emphasis on family honor, can lead to harsh consequences for those who come out. Family rejection, disownment, and even violence are common experiences for LGBTQ+ Iraqis.

While Iraqi Kurdistan is often perceived as a more tolerant region, LGBTQ+ individuals still face significant challenges and risks there. Societal stigma, family honour codes, and the lack of legal protection can leave LGBTQ+ individuals vulnerable to abuse. The tragic case of Doski Azad, a transgender woman who was killed by her brother on 28 January 2022, highlights the ongoing dangers faced by LGBTQ+ individuals in the region. The media's reluctance to cover these issues due to fear of harassment is a significant obstacle to raising awareness and advocating for change.

The lack of clear laws against perpetrators of LGBTQ+ killings in Iraq, coupled with the tendency of authorities to frame these crimes as 'honour killings,' or family disputes, creates a climate of impunity that allows perpetrators to evade justice. The absence of specific laws criminalising violence against LGBTQ+ individuals, combined with social and cultural pressures, and the prevalence of corruption within the legal system, can hinder efforts to hold perpetrators accountable. The formation of so-called investigation committees in these cases often serves as a tactic to delay justice and potentially cover up the crimes, particularly in a context where public attention is quickly drawn to new events and scandals. When LGBTQ+ individuals in Iraq attempt to report these incidents to authorities, they may be detained without any reason or subjected to sexual exploitation.

Numerous factors compel Iraqi youth, including LGBTQ+ individuals, to migrate abroad. The pervasive insecurity, limited job opportunities, and political instability within Iraq create a challenging environment for many. For LGBTQ+ individuals, the additional threat of discrimination and persecution exacerbates their situation.

In Iraq, securing employment in both the private and public sectors can be challenging. However, LGBTQ+ individuals face even greater obstacles due to discrimination during the job-seeking process. Even if they manage to find employment, LGBTQ+ individuals often experience discrimination, verbal abuse, and a hostile work environment. This lack of societal acceptance forces many to conceal their identities or present themselves in ways that contradict their true selves.

Turkey and Lebanon have emerged as popular destinations for these migrants. Turkey, a geographically proximate country with a comparatively liberal stance on LGBTQ+ rights in the Middle East, often serves as a first stop for those seeking asylum or a better life. Lebanon, while facing its own challenges, is generally considered more LGBTQ+ friendly within the Arab world, offering some degree of acceptance and tolerance.

The year 2015 witnessed a significant migration wave from Iraq and other countries towards Europe. Thousands of individuals, including members of the LGBTQ+ community, embarked on perilous journeys by sea in search of a safer and more accepting life. The decision by Turkish authorities to open the sea door to migrants seeking to reach Europe provided a unique opportunity for many, including LGBTQ+ individuals, to escape the challenges and discrimination they faced in their home countries. These individuals carried with them dreams of a better life, often seeking countries that would recognise their rights and provide the freedom they had been denied.

Iraq's conservative society continues to restrict LGBTQ+ individuals from freely expressing themselves in public. They remain under the control of family, community, and religious beliefs, which can pose significant threats to their lives if they choose to 'come out.' LGBTQ+ individuals in Iraq often face difficulties in seeking help from their families or local communities when encountering problems on dating apps. The lack of community acceptance and protective laws further complicates their ability to address the challenges they face.

In early 2024, the Iraqi parliament passed amendments to a law criminalising homosexuality. The revised law increased the maximum sentence for homosexuals to 15 years. Additionally, transgender individuals now face imprisonment of one to three years. The legislation also criminalises promoting homosexuality or prostitution, performing sex reassignment surgery, and individuals who 'imitate' women or engage in wife swapping.

Iraq faces a significant lack of non-governmental organisations advocating for LGBTQ+ rights. Even existing organisations may face restrictions under the new law, which prohibits any activities promoting LGBTQ+ rights. Human rights organisations in Iraq often operate under repressive conditions and under the threat of being closed down. As a result, many of these organisations have resorted to online activism, or work from outside the country. Notable organisations working in this area include IraQueer; which aims to raise awareness about the LGBTQ+ community in Iraq and the Kurdistan Region.

The October 2019 protests in Iraq were a watershed moment for the country, as well as marking a significant turning point for LGBTQ+ rights advocates. Thousands of Iraqis, driven by frustration with widespread corruption, lack of services, and economic hardship, took to the streets to demand change. Amidst the broader demonstrations against corruption and government inefficiency, many LGBTQ+ individuals found a platform to voice their concerns and demand greater acceptance and equality.

While LGBTQ+ people in Iraq have awareness and culture, and mastery of ways to participate in peaceful demonstrations, their participation in demonstrations did not carry slogans or special flags or any indication of their identity for fear of being attacked and targeted by armed groups. They went out to the streets to express their desire to overthrow the corrupt authority that came after the US occupation of Iraq after 2003.

In a powerful act of defiance, some LGBTQ+ individuals in Baghdad have painted their hands with the rainbow flag and taken photos in public squares. This bold statement is a message to both the community and the authorities, that they are here, visible, and demand recognition as integral members of society. By displaying the rainbow flag, they are calling for legal recognition and protection, hoping to create a more inclusive and peaceful environment for all.

LGBTQ+ individuals in many countries worldwide commemorate Pride Month with public marches and celebrations. Most European authorities provide full protection for these events. However, in Arab countries like Iraq, Pride celebrations are limited to small, secretive gatherings. LGBTQ+ individuals in Iraq lack the right to publicly celebrate or express their identities, and such gatherings are illegal.

Followers of the social media LGBTQ+ groups in Iraq mostly use pseudonyms to participate in celebrations of Pride Month online. This fear of being identified by family, friends, or authorities has led them to take precautions to protect their privacy and avoid harassment, threats, arrest, or imprisonment.

Government and militia members are infiltrating popular gay dating apps, primarily Grindr, with malicious intent. Online hate speech against LGBTQ+ individuals has surged, particularly from political and religious figures. Iraqi Shiite cleric Muqtada Al-Sadr has repeatedly claimed that monkeypox is caused by homosexuality. His statements have been widely embraced by his millions of followers across Iraq, while activists, NGOs, and human rights centres have strongly condemned them as a dangerous threat to the people of the LGBTQ+ community. Al-Sadr has even proposed designating a day for anti-homosexual sentiments.

Al-Sadr's social media posts have been notorious for their inconsistency and volatility. While he has occasionally expressed support for ending violence against LGBTQ+ individuals, garnering praise from local and international organisations, he has frequently contradicted himself. For example, Al-Sadr blamed the LGBTQ+ community for the COVID-19 pandemic, claiming it was a result of legalising same-sex marriage in Western countries. These dangerous statements hold significant weight due to Al-Sadr's ability to command immediate obedience from millions of followers.

LGBTQ+ individuals worldwide use dating apps to connect and find partners. While these apps can facilitate relationships and break down barriers, they also pose risks, particularly in countries like Iraq. One such risk is the infiltration of these apps by individuals who are not part of the LGBTQ+ community. These individuals may use dating apps to target and harm community members. Examples of such apps include Grindr and Tinder. Many LGBTQ+ individuals in Iraq avoid sharing personal information during the dating process due to fear of being identified by friends or relatives who may use the same app.

While dating apps can be beneficial, some members of the LGBTQ+ community in Iraq find certain apps, like Grindr, to be toxic environments. These apps may contain individuals who are not part of the community and engage in discriminatory or insulting behaviour. This can negatively impact the mental health of LGBTQ+ individuals. Many LGBTQ+ people are hesitant to use their real photos or provide accurate personal information on dating apps due to safety concerns. Civil organisations advise caution when interacting with strangers on dating apps, suggesting that individuals take time to get to know each other and understand each other's perspectives on the LGBTQ+ community.

LGBTQ+ individuals in Iraq however often find dating apps valuable, even when not seeking romantic relationships. These apps can provide a way to connect with others, make friends, and build relationships. For many in the LGBTQ+ community, who may struggle to integrate into mainstream society, dating apps, when used with precautions, offer a space to feel comfortable and safe.

Many Iraqi political parties have played a negative role by criticising homosexuality. Additionally, demonstrations protesting the burning of the Quran in Sweden and Denmark, which included the burning of rainbow flags, have further fuelled hostility towards the LGBTQ+ community. These incidents have created a threatening environment for LGBTQ+ individuals and incited hate speech, prompting many to avoid social media to protect themselves.

In May 2024, the KRG Court ordered the closure of Rasan, a human rights organisation in the Kurdistan Region of Iraq, due to its advocacy for LGBTQ+ rights.

In August 2024, the Iraqi Communications and Media Commission issued a directive banning the use of the terms 'gender' and 'homosexuality' in all media outlets.

LGBTQ+ individuals incarcerated in Iraqi prisons often face abuse and exploitation by security personnel and guards. These individuals are left isolated and without adequate psychological or material support. Their families may be hesitant to visit prisons due to the fear of being forced to witness their suffering. LGBTQ+ inmates face discrimination from both fellow inmates and prison staff. To avoid further abuse and violations of their rights, some LGBTQ+ individuals may be coerced into making sexual concessions to security personnel.

In July 2017, Karrar Noshi, an actor and graduate of a Baghdad Fine Arts Institute, was tragically killed armed groups in Baghdad because he looked gay. Despite the crime, those responsible remain unidentified and unaccountable.

The blogger Noor Al-Saffar, known as Noor BM was fatally shot in Baghdad by a gunman on a food delivery motorcycle, in September 2023. His death sparked outrage among human rights organisations and activists in Iraq. Prior to this, the popular Instagram influencer Hamoudi Al-Mutairi, believed to be 14 years old, was stabbed to death near his home in Baghdad, in an apparent homophobic attack by youths who believed he was gay.

The systematic killing of LGBTQ+ individuals, exemplified by the tragic case of Hamoudi Al-Mutairi, persists. Perpetrators continue to evade justice and remain free, leaving a climate of fear and impunity.

During the occupation of large parts of Iraq in June 2016, Islamic State in Iraq and Syria (ISIS) implemented its own militant interpretation of Islamic law. Homosexuality was considered a severe crime punishable by harsh penalties. One common punishment for suspected homosexuals was being thrown from a high building. If the victim survived the fall, ISIS members would then stone them to death. In areas without high-rise buildings, ISIS resorted to other brutal methods to kill LGBTQ+ individuals.

ISIS used brutal methods to execute LGBTQ+ individuals in Mosul during their occupation in 2014. These included torture, weapons, and stoning. Due to the harsh punishments inflicted by ISIS, some LGBTQ+ individuals were forced to join the group to protect themselves and their families. Others were compelled to report their LGBTQ+ acquaintances to gain favour with ISIS members and secure protection and privileges not available to ordinary citizens.

A local resident, Mustafa Hashim, shared a story with me passed down from his grandfather about the 'dancers.' These young men, renowned for their extraordinary beauty, adorned themselves with ornaments and make-up and performed at celebrations and weddings. More than just dancers, they represented beauty and femininity in a patriarchal society. Tribal leaders protected them, viewing them as valuable additions to their gatherings.

This was not solely a male phenomenon. In the marshes, Hashim told me there was also the 'tomboy,' a woman who defied traditional gender expectations. She cut her hair, participated in men's activities, and even engaged in combat. Additionally, there was the 'transvestite,' a man who chose to live as a woman.

These practices, once deeply ingrained in the marsh culture, gradually declined over time. With the spread of Islamic ideology and the enforcement of stricter traditions, these practices became taboo and condemned. Many of these stories have been lost, and countless individuals have been denied the opportunity to express their authentic selves.

Deep within the swaying reeds of the Iraqi marshes, a unique way of life flourished for centuries. This rarely discussed culture was passed down through generations in hushed whispers. It was a world where men could dress as women, women challenged traditional roles, and society embraced difference, albeit within certain boundaries.

Interviews

Sarah, 28, Baghdad

My name is Sarah. I'm a 28-year-old lesbian from Baghdad. I'm a skilled software engineer and graphic designer.

Twenty-eight years might not seem like much, but I have packed a lot into it. Life has thrown me some curveballs, but I have managed to keep my head above water and steer my ship in the right direction.

Since 2003, my family and I have been nomads, moving from one country to another, one city to the next. My dad's job took us all over Iraq, and we would have to settle into a new place, make new friends, and then say goodbye all over again. It was a crazy ride, but it definitely opened my eyes to different cultures and ways of life.

I spent my childhood bouncing around Syria, Jordan, and the UAE before coming back home to Baghdad in 2012. All that moving around made me wonder who I really was—was I Iraqi, or did my time overseas define me? But around 25, I realised that being Iraqi was a big part of who I am, and it felt really good to finally belong.

My life has been a mix of ups and downs, shaped by my childhood and all the moving around I did. Even though it has not been easy, I'm focused on living a life that is meaningful to me, not just because I'm part of the LGBTQ+ community.

Being LGBTQ+ in Baghdad has not been easy. It's really messed with my life. But I'm trying to move past it and not let it hold me back.

My story is a bit different from most. I remember having my first crush on my English teacher back in middle school. I think I mixed up my respect for her dedication to teaching with something more, maybe because my mum was often away and really strict, so I did not have a lot of emotional support.

Home felt more like a workplace than a cosy space, so I started having feelings for my teacher. I even daydreamed about her, which was really confusing because I was used to praying at home. My family was not super religious, but we did follow some religious traditions.

In middle school, I was not interested in boys. But when I started high school, all my friends were talking about their crushes and sharing contact info. I tried to do the same to fit in, but it was really hard. I realised that being around girls felt different and special. It was like nothing I had ever felt before.

Even though most people in Iraq who study software engineering are men, I decided to go for it anyway. I'm really passionate about it, so I did not let anything stop me.

In my first year of college, I was interested in a guy, not romantically, but because he was really nice and loyal. I tried to fit in with him, but eventually, I realised that I did not see myself in a relationship with him because I only have feelings for women. So, we decided to just be friends.

I kept trying to make things work with guys, both online and in person. I would go on dates and even try to get physical, but nothing ever clicked. It felt forced and unnatural. I started to wonder what was wrong with me. Then it hit me: when I'm around women, it's a whole different story. There is a real connection and attraction that I do not feel with men.

Maybe I'm not straight? Maybe I'm somewhere on the LGBTQ+ spectrum? It's confusing, but also really interesting! Luckily, there are tons of resources to help me figure it out. I might check out some online forums or try a dating app for LGBTQ+ people. Who knows, maybe I will finally meet someone who I really connect with, someone who makes my heart race for the right reasons. This is about finding a real connection, and I'm finally ready to do it my way. It might take a while, but the journey itself could be amazing.

In 2016, I met an exceptional woman online. She was not from Baghdad, but her bravery was what truly captivated me. Her courage and strength were inspiring, and I was immediately drawn to her unique personality.

In recent years, I have begun to question the societal norms and expectations placed upon me. My appearance, interests, and actions may not always align with my true self.

For a long time, I kept my sexual orientation hidden. My family saw me as someone who conformed to societal norms, dressing 'normally' and presenting a traditional appearance. But underneath, a part of me yearned for freedom. Gradually, I began to express myself more authentically, starting with small changes like wearing comfortable clothes. My parents noticed and commented: "You look like a boy."

I do not deny my feminine side; it's as real to me as the air I breathe. However, society often insists on rigid gender roles, expecting boys to be responsible and behave in a certain way, and girls to conform to different expectations. Caught between these two worlds, I have struggled to find my place.

Throughout this journey, I have sought out supportive communities—friends who celebrate my individuality and online spaces where I can connect with others on similar paths. Their support and encouragement remind me that I'm not alone. While there are moments of doubt and inner turmoil, I have learned to be kind to myself.

In social situations, I have noticed a pattern: women often wait for men to take the initiative. But I have always been proactive. Whether we were at a restaurant or making important life decisions, I enjoy taking the lead.

People often assume I'm playing a masculine role, and some make assumptions about my personal life. For example, some believe I'm not romantically involved with a man because of my strong or assertive demeanour. I avoid serious conversations with them because it's difficult for them to understand or accept that I'm acting this way as a lesbian. In my society, people judge me based on my appearance and behaviour, without considering my inner thoughts and experiences.

My family has recently started reminding my brother that he is not man enough since he allows me to come home late. They claim that it's a brother's responsibility to hold his sister accountable; otherwise, he is not a man in their opinion. Although I do not tell my family about my job or the people I meet, I have to be cautious. For example, I cannot say "This is my friend" but rather "my colleague."

In Iraq, the word 'friend' can have multiple meanings, sometimes implying a romantic relationship for societal justification. However, 'colleague' suggests a strictly professional relationship, which is often more acceptable to families. Navigating these cultural nuances can be challenging, and I've had to be particularly careful with my language and behaviour.

My sexual orientation is still hidden from my family and friends. Sometimes my brother jokes with me and says, "I think you might be a lesbian." I make excuses and tell him that I'm in love with a man. In these situations, I pretend to have a crush on someone and show him photos of my friend, who is actually just a friend. This is the only way to keep his suspicions at bay. I only have one woman friend who knows everything about me, and is supportive. At first, she was not accepting of me being a lesbian, but she eventually became supportive and even gave me advice on relationships and how to act in different situations.

At work, I have become close to a gay colleague. While we are not romantically attracted to each other, we are considering getting married to hide our sexual orientations from our families and society. I realise this is a complex decision, and I'm still weighing the pros and cons. While I cannot imagine having a romantic or sexual relationship with a man, this arrangement could offer a degree of safety and acceptance within our society.

In Iraq, girls, including myself, have limited options for dating and meeting people. Social media platforms like Instagram, Twitter, and Tinder are popular for communication. On Tinder, I often connect with girls and talk with them. However, there are risks involved, as some young men create fake female accounts to target girls. I'm not sure what their intentions are, but they likely want to identify lesbian women and sometimes extort them for money or sex using information and pictures they have obtained.

Once, I was blackmailed by someone I thought was a girl. I was threatened with extortion for money. I reached out to a friend who works for a government security authority, who helped me address the problem. I've also received anonymous communications informing me that they knew I was a lesbian, and intended to intimidate me or damage my reputation at work, in society, and among friends. I responded by blocking them and being more cautious in my online interactions.

I live in constant fear because I'm a girl who chooses to live freely, even though I continue to hide my sexual orientation from everyone. My only option is to emigrate and leave my homeland in order to live and express myself authentically. I'm currently trying to save money to relocate to another country and cover my living expenses there.

I have considered telling my family about my sexual orientation, but I find it difficult to come out because I don't want to shock them or cause psychological harm. I'm not sure how they will react, but I'm afraid they will feel terrible.

Boha, 27, Baghdad

You can call me Boha, not my real name for safety concerns. I'm a 27-year-old gay man from Baghdad. I have spent most of my life in Baghdad with my family, which includes my parents and three sisters. I lived in Turkey for a year and returned to Iraq, where I currently work as a human resources specialist in a private company.

I spent my childhood in Bab Al-Sheikh, a beloved neighbourhood in Baghdad that holds a special place in my heart. I was born there, and even though my family moved to another neighbourhood when I was one, I often return to visit. My father used to work there, so we still have some connections to this place.

As the only son, I was the spoiled child of the family, receiving a lot of attention, especially from my father. He would buy me anything I wanted. Unfortunately, my father passed away when I was eleven. After that, I began to feel a growing sense of responsibility towards my family, particularly my sisters. I took on some of the responsibilities my father had previously carried, though my mother shouldered the majority of the burden of raising my sisters in a society that is particularly challenging for girls without a father.

My school years were somewhat stable, but they were certainly not free from challenges. I faced bullying from my classmates due to my overweight, which significantly impacted my mentality in my childhood. In a culture where the strong dominate the weak, I was a vulnerable target. While I started socialising with other students in middle and high school, I felt disconnected from their conversations about relationships with girls. I did not feel a part of that world, and I realised my feelings were different from theirs. Although I did not fully understand my sexuality at the time, I knew I was not straight.

I started to understand myself better around the age of nineteen, including my sexual orientation and gender identity. Even though I had past experiences of relationships and physical intimacy, I did not fully understand myself until I started reading and learning more about gender and sexuality. Accepting myself has been a journey, and there have been times when I have struggled with self-doubt. However, I have come to accept who I am. In fact, I have known I was not straight since I was eight years old.

Being gay in Iraq is so risky. The mere suspicion of one's true identity can lead to severe consequences. I have spent my life masking my sexuality, pretending to be straight. Despite my best efforts, people often sense that I'm not straight—oh, that is true! It's a constant balancing act: living a lie to survive while yearning for authenticity.

Back in my school days, during high school, I admired a classmate. I can only assume that he knew I was gay. He was a close friend, but after high school, he disappeared, and I lost contact with him. I suspected he might be gay or bisexual himself, but his extreme religious beliefs seemed to conflict with his true identity. Despite knowing I was gay, he urged me to pray and adhere to Islamic principles, claiming it would 'cure' my homosexuality. He considered my sexual orientation sinful and a source of divine anger. Now, I fear he may have joined an extremist group like ISIS due to his so very Islamic extremism ideology.

The other person I admired, and who admired me in return, was my cousin. This mutual admiration began in 2017. However, he lacked awareness about sexuality, prioritising sexual relationships over emotional connections. He has experienced a hard family issue that made him change his perspective on relationships with young men, considering such relationships as taboo and something to be avoided. This shift likely stemmed from societal pressures. Despite this, I believe he still harbours feelings for me, as evidenced by his gaze when we meet.

My family was suspicious of our relationship due to his reputation as a playboy. However, as cousins, it was easy for us to visit each other's homes without raising eyebrows. When he moved to my neighbourhood, our interactions increased, further fuelling suspicions. However, we still connected to each other but under the friendship limit and within the relatives' ties. My parents were aware of the scrutiny, though no one explicitly voiced their concerns to me. While they were aware of my sexual orientation, they seemed to prefer avoiding raising the topic.

As an LGBTQ+ person in Iraq, I face numerous challenges daily. The most significant being the inability to publicly express my true identity. This feeling leads to internal struggles and external challenges.

At work, I must pretend to be straight, navigating interactions with colleagues cautiously. My position as HR specialist, which requires frequent contact with employees, further complicates this. To avoid potential repercussions, I must hide my true self and adopt a character that aligns with societal expectations, limiting my authenticity and ability to be who I truly am.

My masculine appearance helps me blend in and avoid suspicion. It's unfortunate that society often associates homosexuality with feminine traits, a harmful stereotype. This prejudice makes it difficult for LGBTQ+ individuals to find employment, as many employers are hesitant to hire those who do not conform to traditional gender norms. It's a discriminatory practice, that denies individuals their fundamental rights based on sexual orientation or what a person looks like.

"When did you get married?" is a common question in Iraqi society, particularly for men who have achieved job stability or reached adulthood. My family, relatives, and friends often inquire about marriage plans or offer to help find a suitable wife. This tradition, while fading in some areas, remains prevalent in many parts of Iraq.

My family constantly asks me about marriage. I have been using my plan to study for a master degree or to improve my career position as excuses to delay it, but last year, they hinted at finding a wife for me. I refused, and now they have stopped asking. But, if not my family, others will inevitably ask, "When did you get married?"

Until a few years after 2003, there were no social media or dating apps for gay people in Iraq. During my adolescence, meeting and getting to know others who share my interests was extremely difficult. Meetings were limited to a close circle of friends who lived in the same neighbourhood. Even after the spread of social media and dating apps years later, when meeting people became easier, it remained fraught with danger.

During my final year of university, a gay friend there introduced me to Grindr, that was in 2018, but I did not use this app until 2021. Intrigued by the prospect of connecting with others, I downloaded it, hoping to find trustworthy people, and potentially a partner. However, my expectations were quickly challenged. While the app offered new opportunities, many users seemed primarily interested in casual dating with many different people. I was seeking something more serious—a genuine connection and a lasting relationship.

Grindr's focus on physical appearance was another negative aspect. Users often prioritised specific body types over deeper qualities like personality, culture, and values. This superficial approach initially motivated me to change my appearance, leading me to the gym. While I initially worked out to fit societal expectations, I eventually realised that self-improvement should be for personal fulfilment, not external validation. Despite my efforts, I discovered that many on the app were primarily interested in superficial connections, highlighting the app's limitations in fostering meaningful relationships.

Returning to university life, I recall a particularly impactful moment that has stayed with me. I entered a university bathroom and noticed a phrase written on the wall: 'I am gay.' This simple message resonated with me deeply. Until then, I had felt isolated, believing I was the only LGBTQ+ person in the country. The illogical thought had hindered my self-confidence.

Seeing that phrase, however, was a turning point. It made me realise I was not alone. I felt a sense of support, recognition, and acceptance of my identity. As I walked away, tears streamed down my face. From that day forward, I began to embrace my gayness with greater confidence.

In late 2023, I decided to stop using the LGBTQ+ dating apps. I found myself unsatisfied with the experiences and connections I was making. I was not finding the kind of people I wanted to get to know, or any potential for a long-term relationship. Instead, I focused on building friendships at work. I enjoy spending time with these friends and value the genuine connections we have formed.

I had a frightening experience on Grindr. After sharing personal information and photos with someone I met on the app, he began to threaten to blackmail me by ruining my reputation in society. His aggressive behaviour seemed to stem from his own personal issues, or perhaps his hate towards the LGBTQ+ community.

To calm the situation, I apologised and falsely claimed that being gay is a sin. Unfortunately, this did not deter him. As a last resort, I called the authorities to report the blackmail attempt. However, the person who took my call offered no help and blamed me for using this app. Thank God, he just blamed me! Looking back, I realise contacting a government agency was not the best solution, and risky. At the time, I was desperate to protect my reputation in a society that stigmatises LGBTQ+ individuals.

After everything I have been through, I believe that Iraqis urgently need specialised psychological support centres for LGBTQ+ individuals. These centres would provide crucial mental health care and a safe space for those facing daily discrimination and prejudice. However, given the Iraqi government's criminalisation of homosexuality, the establishment of such centres seems unlikely.

Abdullah, 33, Baghdad

I'm Abdullah, a 33-year-old gay man living in Baghdad. The city is deeply ingrained in my identity. I grew up here with my family—my parents and two sisters. We lived in a neighbourhood with narrow, winding streets. I have fond memories of playing there as a child. However, as I matured, I started to feel different. I realised I was gay. It was a secret because being gay is not accepted in Baghdad or the rest of Iraq.

My childhood was challenging. I was afraid of how my family and friends might react, so I kept my feelings and identity hidden.

Despite my dreams and aspirations, wars, sectarian tensions, and economic hardship forced me to abandon my education and find work to support my family.

Leaving school was a difficult decision, but I knew I needed to be strong and determined. I missed the daily routine of carrying my bag and attending classes, but life, it seems, is full of unexpected turns.

As a child, it was difficult to find suitable employment. However, I had to. While searching for work, I practiced my talent in my small room. I bought pencils with money I saved to start drawing. When I draw, I can escape the problems outside. I draw beautiful places, bustling cities, and even imaginary animals, or people I know or do not know. In my drawings, I can imagine a world where anything is possible. Even the bad things can have a glimmer of hope.

I have always been curious about the world. I read a lot of books to learn new things, even though I was not in school. Mostly I read books on human development so that I could be stronger and handle the difficult things in my life. However, responsibilities piled up, forcing me to trade long hours at work for stolen moments of sleep. My haven of learning became a distant memory. The ache for knowledge still lingers. I miss getting lost in a book, the symphony of a new melody taking shape on paper.

I know finding time will not be easy, but even a small amount dedicated to these passions each week is essential. Perhaps online courses, a book club with like-minded people, or volunteering at social events could be the key. Somehow, I will find a way to reignite that flame of learning. This vast and ever-changing world deserves to be explored, one discovery at a time.

Work came early for me. At just seven years old, I found myself in a small woodshop, helping out a carpenter. The work was physically demanding, and by the end of the day my body ached. Using tools and shaping wood sparked something in me. Fast forward to 2003, and I was helping out a tailor who made military uniforms. Cutting fabric and threading needles was not glamorous, but it taught me precision and focus. These jobs, starting when I was just a kid, revealed a lot about who I am. I could handle hard work, follow directions, and take responsibility. But they also presented challenges.

One of my first stops was a women's clothing store in Baghdad's Shorja Market. I spent a long time there selling clothes. Every day, I carried the weight of my worries and aspirations on my shoulders. My future felt uncertain, and my dreams seemed out of reach, especially in a country where I felt stifled and unable to express myself or pursue my long-held goals.

Now, I work at a car parts store. It's a daily grind, but I have grown to enjoy it. Earning $15 a day is not much, but it's a step towards stability and fulfilling my dreams. Despite the challenges, I have not given up hope. I'm determined to escape my current situation and live openly as myself.

Living in Iraq is incredibly challenging for everyone, given the ongoing security threats and economic hardships. However, these difficulties are exponentially amplified for members of the LGBTQ+ community. We face widespread rejection, fears, and discrimination, and are at risk of persecution, or even death by armed groups.

At work and in public, I must hide my true self. Being gay is both socially and legally prohibited. If my boss knew that I'm gay, I could get fired from work, or even face worse consequences.

At thirteen, I started to realise I was attracted to people of the same sex. However, the wars and chaos in my country made it difficult for me to explore my identity. There was no time or space to think about anything other than survival. I felt isolated and alone, with no one to talk to or share my feelings with.

Being gay and belonging to a Muslim family added another layer of risk. To make things worse, I could not even keep my opinions about politics to myself. My fearless criticism of the political parties and authorities, exposing their corruption and destruction of the country, turned my life into a living nightmare. I was relentlessly harassed, threatened, and persecuted.

During the 2006-2007 sectarian violence, Baghdad was a chaotic war zone. Al-Qaeda terrorists targeted me due to my Shia accent, and I narrowly escaped death. In Shia areas, my Baghdadi accent made me a suspect of being a Sunni spy. Criticising political extremism alienated both Sunni and Shia radicals. To stay safe, I had to move, but the danger never completely disappeared. And as a gay man in Iraq, I felt constantly exposed and at risk at every single moment.

Fleeing the sectarian violence, my family and I moved to the Baghdad suburb Sadr City. It was not exactly utopia, but it's where I met him—my ex, a man six years older than me. At that time, he became a close friend, confidante, lover—he was my protector in a world that felt increasingly hostile.

During our relationship, I was constantly afraid that we might lose each other due to societal restrictions. My ex-boyfriend's parents pressured him to get married, a common practice among Iraqi families when their sons reach a marriageable age. This was a significant reason why our relationship could not continue. So, our relationship ended after eight years. Yes, eight years. Eight years of a love that words just cannot capture. Every time I was in his arms, it felt like a constant, safe haven of comfort. It was a truly special and beautiful relationship. Those moments of pure love and warmth left an undeniable mark on my soul.

He made me feel genuinely confident and happy in a way I never had before. Eight years of shared feelings and unforgotten memories that will forever be a part of me. How lucky am I to have had a partner who filled me with such love and sense of security!

Here I was, wrestling with who I am, and all I could think about was, and still is, staying safe. It was a constant battle, this thing inside of me. I crave acceptance, a place where I can be myself without judgment. But the fear … the fear of rejection, of being cast out … it's a heavy weight to carry.

It's like I'm walking on thin ice. The worst part is the fear of what my family might do. I have heard stories of gays in my city being disowned or even killed for being gay, or even just appearing gay by their looks. The thought of bringing shame to my family and being a target for an honour killing is a constant nightmare. Every day feels like a battle, with danger lurking around every corner.

There was a time in my life when volunteering with local NGOs filled my days. It was not my sole focus, but a significant and enriching part of my existence. I immersed myself in a variety of projects, working alongside passionate individuals who shared my dedication. One day, we offered 'gender equality' training to a select group of youths, and after one of the sessions some people started threatening me. Some threats were said directly to my face, while others were posted online. It was very scary. People threatened me because I spoke out about gender equality and LGBTQ+ rights. These topics are considered taboo in my country. Due to the threats, I had to leave my home and live with a friend for my safety.

When people threatened me directly, I stood up for myself and refused to be scared. When people threatened me indirectly, I reported their actions and blocked them online. The threats I faced became more serious between 2018 and 2020. Once, while walking home in Baghdad, I was attacked by members of Asaib Ahl al-Haq, a militia led by Qais Khazali, who is loyal to Iran. I believe they attacked me because I had criticised their group. Another time, I was threatened for criticising the Sadrist group on social media. Both times, my attackers disappeared without a trace.

In the conservative Iraqi landscape, dating apps like Grindr have become a lifeline for the LGBTQ+ community. Digital platforms offer a rare opportunity for connection, conversation, and even romance. However, the fragile sense of belonging it provides comes with a significant risk.

The app's user base is diverse, attracting individuals from all walks of life, including well-known figures, politicians, military personnel, and even those in positions of power within the judiciary and media. While some users seek genuine companionship, others may harbour malicious intentions.

Those who discover your address or personal information can exploit it for blackmailing. One night, I matched with someone on Grindr. We chatted for a while, but then things took a sinister turn. He claimed to know all about me, saying he had my personal details. He threatened to expose me, to ruin my life. I will not lie—it terrified me. But I refused to give in. I blocked him and shut him out. Even so, the fear lingered for days. That experience only reinforced my desire to leave Iraq, and find a place where I can finally be myself without fear.

Since the successive governments that came to power after 2003, LGBTQ+ individuals have faced increasing persecution. Close friends of mine disappeared during campaigns known as 'physical liquidation.' Our sexual orientation was deemed an abomination by religious and political figures alike. These same figures demanded even harsher punishments, including the criminalisation of homosexuality itself. The message was clear: 'You are not welcome, not tolerated, not even safe.'

The pain was overwhelming. How can one express the loss of so much love, so much life? Words felt inadequate, so I turned to art. My drawings became a way to express the storm raging within me. Each line, each color, was a cry of anguish, a desperate plea for a world where being gay would not be a death sentence.

The dream of reaching the United States or Canada has burned bright in me for years. It's an ambition I share with my friend, and we have been working diligently on legal immigration applications, seeking a better life. For us, it's the only path that feels truly safe. The stories of illegal immigration are terrifying; tales of people losing their lives at sea or somewhere lost in the middle of nowhere during a risky journey. That's a risk I would not dare to take. We decided to do this journey in a legal and safe way, even if it takes time.

The increasing pressure I faced in Iraq made me yearn to leave the country. I attempted to obtain a U.S. Diversity Visa, but was unsuccessful. I also reached out to organisations that support LGBTQ+ individuals, but they could not assist me. I'm still searching for a way to escape and live a safe and free life.

Like many others, I have experienced the dangers of this toxic environment. When I was assaulted, I could not report it to the police because I feared my attacker would retaliate. I do not trust the security forces to protect people's rights. And I'm afraid that if I told the police I'm gay, they might exploit me or put me in jail.

For us, as LGBTQ+ community, imagine what our lives are like. We have no family to protect us, no country to defend us, and everybody else against us.

I'm 34 years old now, and I'm still searching for myself. As a gay man in Iraq, I yearn for love in a safe land, a society that accepts me as I am. What I'm looking for are just basic rightful rights, but for us they remain distant dreams. Nevertheless, I have not lost hope. I'm still fighting with every breath to achieve this dream, to live authentically, to embrace my true self.

My story reflects the experiences of many LGBTQ+ individuals in Iraq. It's not just about me—I'm a voice for the countless others who are silenced.

Laith, 25, Babylon

I call myself Laith, a taken name I use to safeguard myself as I live in a country where being gay at the least is a 'criminal offense' under the law and social customs both. I'm the middle sibling in a family who all live in Babylon.

When I was a young boy, I could not quite put into words the feelings that stirred within me, but I remember, as early as five years old, feeling a certain joyfulness whenever I saw handsome boys on the TV; those were simple times, when the TV was my only window to the vast world outside, long before the internet brought it all right to our doorstep.

As a child, I was draped in the softness of femininity. I keepsake the photographs of my younger self, with long blonde curls and dresses that flowed like an extension of my soul. But as school began, that natural expression was halted; my hair was cut under school rules, and with each cut, it felt as though fragments of who I was were being discarded. It was a deep cut into my being, a wound that remained raw until I stepped out from the shadows of education and into the light of my own truth.

I promised myself, when I join the university I will grow back my lost curls, as university rules are different than the school rules, so, I did, I grew back my nice long hair, to regain a part of me that was once stripped away. It was the start of an unyielding battle against the strict confines society tried to impose on me. I did try to fit in, to weave myself into the fabric of normalcy, but the closer I got, the more intense their gaze became, picking at the seams of my existence. But here I am, standing firm on the path of embracing who I am.

Reflecting on my childhood, I see a tapestry of play woven from the threads of both traditionally feminine and masculine pastimes. I cradled dolls in my arms with the same tenderness that I raced cars across the living room floor. My days were filled with the innocent drama of dress-up and the domestic bliss of playing house, yet they were equally punctuated by the imagined clashes and chaos of action-packed games.

Ah, the tempestuous teenage years—a time when emotions surge like waves crashing upon the shore. Hormones dance, brains rewire, and newfound independence beckons. It's a heady mix, this cocktail of adolescence.

In the quiet of the night, when the rest of the house was lost in dreams, I would find my way to the laptop. That time, Google became my silent partner, the keeper of my secrets. I would enter words like 'male models' and 'handsome boys' and press Enter. The screen would come to life, showcasing the epitome of masculine beauty—sculpted bodies and intense stares that spoke of a world I longed to be part of. This was my private journey, a secret exploration of my desires.

Each image was a window, offering a peek into a realm I was eager to explore and understand. As I navigated through the endless sea of search results, a question lingered in my mind: What existed beyond the confines of the screen? Was it possible for me to close the distance between the digital realm and the tangible world? The answers were as elusive as shadows in the night, yet I knew my quest had only just started. Maybe, just maybe, the understanding I sought would manifest, not through the cold glow of pixels, but in the living, breathing moments of human connection—the gentle pressure of a hand, the tender curve of a smile.

One of those days, a single image would change everything I thought I knew. It showed two men embracing, their lips meeting in a kiss—a powerful depiction that introduced me to the word 'gay.' As I explored further, a chill swept through me. My breathing became rapid, my heart pounded, and a wave of anxiety overwhelmed me. I was in the throes of a panic attack, watching as the conventional future of my family and society restrained me if I lived my entire life in Iraq.

Throughout my teenage years and into early adulthood, I struggled with feelings of self-doubt and resentment. These negative emotions clouded my self-esteem and made it difficult to see my own worth. As a result, I often turned inward, blaming myself for my difficulties. Additionally, I felt alienated from both religious teachings and societal norms, leading to a sense of isolation and frustration.

In my teens, I remember there was a friend at school, a beacon of open-mindedness, who seemed to me a bridge to the wider world I sought to understand. In the depth of my longing for good relations, I took the decision to reveal my true self to him. The day arrived when I gathered my courage and came out. His words cut through me: "That is a curse," he said. My heart sank into an abyss of rejection, but I held fast to my authenticity, responding: "There's nothing I can do about it."

To my surprise, he accepted my truth without judgment, and our friendship remained strong—a testament to the power of genuine connection. However, I became overly cautious of how I expressed myself, afraid of revealing too much.

It was a monumental moment, yet as I continued to come out to others, a profound realisation dawned on me. The act of coming out, time and again, felt insufficient. I was seeking a connection deeper than mere acknowledgment—a bond with someone who understood it innately, who shared the same fabric of being. I longed for a presence when coming out was unnecessary because recognition and understanding were implicit. I yearned for someone to see me, truly see me, because in me, they saw a reflection of themselves.

At eighteen, the weight of my world became unbearable. Depression's shadow loomed large, loneliness became a constant companion, and exhaustion seeped into my bones. Life felt like an endless battle, both within and without, and I was trapped in a limbo, waiting for a real beginning that seemed perpetually out of reach. In my despair, I turned to self-harm, watched my academic performance falter, and one harrowing day, I attempted to end my sufferings. Thankfully, it was not the end. Instead, it marked the start of a new chapter as I sought therapy, a step towards healing and understanding.

In those formative years, the digital world was a distant reality, its presence in our lives measured a mere couple of hours each day. This scarcity of technology became the fertile ground for my creativity to flourish. My imagination was my playground, a realm where the rules were mine to make and every scenario was possible. It was a world where I was free to explore, to be, without the confines of screens. Everything was fair play, and in that freedom, I found the boundless joy of childhood.

My initial encounter with the term 'homosexuality' unfolded through the lens of Islam—an unfortunate introduction, to say the least. I stumbled upon it while reading a book about the signs of doomsday. One of these signs was that those men would adopt women attire and behaviour. The concept baffled me—how could such a transformation occur? Little did I realise that my own childhood play had already blurred those gender lines.

But societal indoctrination ran deep, and I recoiled from the mere thought. It remained etched in my mind as something strange, repulsive even—a puzzle I could not solve.

The familiar societal expectations that had once guided my life crumbled around me. I was left feeling adrift, facing the daunting prospect of starting over. The clear path I had envisioned was now gone, and I braced myself for the unknown challenges that lay ahead, a life less conventional than I had imagined.

In my struggle with conflicting thoughts, I found comfort in what I had always known. I immersed myself in the religious teachings of my youth, hoping to find peace. My days became a series of prayers, the mosque's halls resonated with my presence, and the Quran was never far from my side. I was trying to change an integral part of myself through faith, believing it could resolve the turmoil within me. But now, as I share my story, it's clear that such efforts cannot change who I fundamentally am.

Time, often called the silent healer, indeed has the gentle power to smooth out life's roughest edges. In recent times, I have felt the tempest of my resentment quiet down, replaced by a calm I have yearned for. The intense hatred that once filled me is fading, leaving a void, but also room for new growth. It's a delicate peace I am carefully tending to, fostering it with the hope that, in time, it will flourish into a future where acceptance is not just possible, but thrives.

It was a few years back that I began to pen my thoughts, crafting blogs on a myriad of subjects, ranging from the intricacies of business to the boundless realms of art. To be honest with you, writing have become my world!

I was diving into writing and reading more on various topics, including LGBTQ+ and advocacy of equal rights; that concept was foreign to me, such things had never been part of my life's education. The notion that I, too, deserved rights—that I was entitled to them simply by virtue of being a human—was a revelation, or like reaching my American Dream.

That feeling was like a powerful awakening to me, a realisation that I'm part of a larger narrative, one where every individual's rights were worth fighting for. Witnessing the vibrant colours of LGBTQ+ pride marches and listening to the anthemic beats of Lady Gaga's 'Born This Way,' a sense of belonging started to stir within me. Her music was like a clarion call for self-acceptance, resonated deeply, and I found myself drawn into the fold of her fandom. There, I encountered others who shared my journey, a community united by a common narrative of self-discovery and advocacy.

In a moment of clarity, I asked myself: "If they are advocating for me, why am I not advocating for myself?" It was a pivotal question that shifted my perspective. I realised that the hatred I had harboured within needed a new direction. No longer could I allow it to consume me from the inside. So, I redirected it outward, towards the societal constructs that had long suppressed voices like mine. It was time to stand up, not just in solidarity with others, but as an advocate for my own right to exist freely and authentically, to be me, the one who I am now.

In my city, the understanding and acceptance I sought were as elusive as shadows at dusk. The online world offered a semblance of what I craved, but it was a mere echo of the connection I yearned for. Despite coming out to numerous people, the void remained unfilled. I longed for romance, for someone to look at me with the same affection I saw in countless films and TV shows. Yet, that chapter of my life remained unwritten, and as I reflect on those years, the absence of that experience lingers as a poignant regret.

In the fragile time between my darkest moment and the first steps toward healing, I chose to reveal my truth to my father. The words I spoke were not mere syllables; they landed with the force of a bullet. His reaction was visceral—a flinch, a hand to his chest—as if the words themselves had wounded him. He turned pale, the colour draining from his face, and in his eyes, I saw a turmoil that mirrored my own.

For days he wrestled with sleepless nights, and in his search for answers, he turned to the familiar solace of religion. He drew me into his orbit, back to the mosque, back to the rituals and prayers that once offered me comfort. But this time, it was different. I was not a willing participant, but a son acquiescing to his father's newfound desperation to understand, to fix, to save. We spent more time together than we had in years, talking about everything and nothing, skirting around the chasm that my confession had opened between us. It was a dance of love and fear, acceptance and denial, as we both grappled with a reality that neither of us was prepared for.

Unburdening myself to my dad was not exactly the emotional breakthrough I had hoped for. But hey, at least it lit a fire under him to get me into therapy. Finding a therapist, though? That was a whole other story. Here I was, walking around with a roadmap of scars etched on my arm from a suicide attempt, not to mention the countless battle wounds scattered across my body—self-inflicted reminders of darker days.

It was like going from doctor to doctor with a band-aid on a gaping wound. They would offer prescriptions or platitudes about prayer, but nothing that truly addressed the storm brewing inside me. Finally, we found him. A therapist, a godsend, who specialised in something called cognitive-behavioural therapy. He did not shy away from the scars, physical or mental. He taught me ways to manage my thoughts and emotions, to break free from the patterns that were dragging me down. It was not about erasing who I was, but building a stronger, healthier me.

I battled a triple threat: clinical depression, anxiety, and a personality disorder. Medication became part of my routine, but it was not the only answer. My journey was about picking myself up, piece by piece, and reaching the dream of joining the university.

University of Baghdad was my escape. It promised a community I craved, a world away from my hometown's suffocating silence. Arriving at 19, I was brimming with self-acceptance, only to be met with a harsh reality. Many in this community, even older members, seemed stuck in a cycle of immaturity and danger. Dates turned into declarations of love, followed by unsettling displays of stalking. It was not the haven I had envisioned.

Many Iraqi LGBTQ+ persons I had met, their life shaped by lack of proper sexual education, painted a different picture of love than the fairytale I craved. The campus would not offer a happily ever after, but it would gift me something far more precious: my chosen family. These were not just friends; they saw the real me, understood me without a word. We were a tribe, bound by shared struggles and unwavering support. Years later, that bond remains unbreakable. We were there for each other, a safety net that catches us when we stumble.

For a long time, the internet was my only sanctuary. I hid behind a fake name and profile picture on social media, pouring my heart out in dark humor. It was a way to laugh at the pain, to make light of my struggles with mental health and identity. But even in the laughter, there was a yearning to be seen. Maybe that is why I had so many friends on that covert account. One day, I took a chance. I swapped the mask for my real face, made my profile public, and started sharing the unfiltered me. It was terrifying, but liberating.

But the fragile safety net I had built shattered. One day, a relative stumbled upon my profile and tattled to my dad. Even though he already knew about my identity, such disapproval fuelled his anger. He demanded I take down the account. Deleting it felt like ripping away a lifeline. It was the only space where I could be myself, laugh at the darkness, and connect with others who understood. Now, that solace was gone, replaced by a deeper depression.

Dad's reaction fuelled a new fire within me: the desperate need for a real safe space, a place where I could exist openly without fear. There were not cafes buzzing with LGBTQ+ life, no parks where couples could hold hands freely. In this city, Babylon, there was not a single space where I could be myself completely.

Right now, my safe space is a curated corner of Instagram. Close Friends Stories let me share with a chosen circle, the people who understand and will not judge.

Art became my sanctuary—a realm where masculine and feminine energies danced in harmony. Brush strokes and ink flowed from my fingertips, transcending the binary. I sculpted my identity, chiselling away shame. The scissors that once severed my curls now shaped my destiny. Each stroke whispered, 'You are more than the sum of your parts.' And so, my journey continued— from playing pretend to crafting visual poetry. I explored art forms, wrote verses, and painted emotions.

Art has always been my voice, a way to express myself freely. After graduation, during the gap year, I felt a deep pull to reconnect with the artistic child I once was, the one before school pressure and life's storms. I grew my hair long again, dusted off my paints and notebooks, and dove back into everything that sparked joy. It was about reclaiming my passions, expressing myself with a fierceness I had not known before. By nurturing that inner child, I rediscovered my autonomy and unleashed a creativity that flowed freely. Everything that came from that reconnection was positive, a testament to the power of embracing my true self.

Does my art have LGBTQ+ themes? It can. But for me, the bigger picture is about self-expression. As someone who has fought to find my voice, every piece I create feels like an act of defiance. It's a reclamation of my story, a way of shouting my truth to the world. Whether it's joy, anger, or quiet contemplation, my art comes from the core of who I am—a proud member of the LGBTQ+ community. And in that way, it's a celebration of the self, a testament to the power of finding my voice.

In 2024, the Iraqi parliament passed an anti-LGBTQ+ law, so, I wrote a poem about this law, it's a visual poem, based on the following lines in English:

What if this is it?
We keep waiting for the right time
Till we get knocked down by the next hit
If we are all children of God then every stillborn
in this cursed home must be God's favourite
Yet we live on day by day by day by day until we are at our wits

What if this is it?
What if that is all we got
Here we make love in the shadows in the dark underground until we rot
Here, I'll think of you every second every day
For they cannot crucify me for my thoughts
Here Cupid's arrow is a death sentence
I tell him, "Take your best shot"
What If that is all we got

What if there is nothing more
What if me making him laugh behind a screen is me raging war
The stories end before they start mourning the lives we never got to
                                                                  explore
What if that is all we're living for?
Are you scared to ask for more?
Cause I'm not scared of jack shit
I'm only scared to admit
What if this is it?

Sharing the video, which illustrate my poem, even with just a private link felt nerve-wracking. It's tough to express myself freely when I have to worry about who is watching. So, I created this online safe space where I can create without judgment. But honestly, it feels like a closed door.

But for now, I'm creating for whoever is willing to listen without judgment. And even if those people are few right now, I know my audience is out there. My poems, my videos, they are seeds I am planting, waiting for the day they find fertile ground.

Another visual poem, 'The 100 Pigeons,' delves into a deeply personal experience—my first encounter with that someone who would take my virginity, but then could not accept himself, and got married with a woman just to pleasure the society and his family. It left lasting scars, a violation symbolised by the constant feeling of being watched, stalked, and surveilled.

What happened to me is illustrated in the visual poem by one hundred origami pigeons, crafted from paper, that hang suspended from my ceiling fan. They surround me, a physical manifestation of that past experience.

But within the vulnerability lies a spark of defiance. Some of the pigeons tilt upwards, their wings outstretched, yearning for escape. The colours are vibrant, a stark contrast to the darkness of the memory. This is my way of reclaiming the space that was once invaded, transforming the symbol of surveillance into a symbol of hope and healing.

I was never pressured to marry by my family, which was a stark contrast to the experiences of many others. But I still had to be very clear about it. Every time the topic came up, I was firm, even forceful, in my refusal. Marriage and children simply were not part of my life plan.

My focus was on escaping these limitations. The economic pressures here are suffocating, and all I crave is the freedom to leave. I have made it abundantly clear—Laith (my pseudo-name) will not be following the traditional path.

Escaping feels like the only breath I have ever known. Every waking moment since I was 18 has been focused on that goal. Learning English, volunteering, excelling in school, building a career—it's all a meticulously crafted path to immigration. Here, in this borrowed cage I have built, I exist. But my real life, the one where I can truly breathe, waits on the other side. It's a harsh reality, not a choice.

Having parents who understood me feels like a missing shield against the world. Safety, in my mind, meant having someone in my corner, someone to confide in during dark times. Imagine having someone to talk to about those moments of physical and emotional hurt, someone who would not judge but offer support and guidance. That is the kind of parental bond I have always craved, a safe harbour in the storm.

Left to navigate those experiences alone, I relied on whatever knowledge I had, even if it was not enough. It left scars, for sure, but recently I have begun the healing process. It's a testament to my strength that I was able to move forward despite the damage.

Hayden, 22, Najaf

My name is Hayden, I'm a 22-year-old queer. I was born and raised in Najaf City, one of the holiest Shia Islamic cities in Iraq and the world. My life was not easy living in a city where religion permeated every aspect. Strict religious rules were imposed on both women and men. Women are forbidden to remove their hijab and men are forbidden to wear short shorts, and other laws restrict many other aspects of personal freedom. Imagine what it would be like for someone who is queer. Guess how my life is.

I identify as queer. I reject any stereotypes about people based on their clothing, accessories, speech patterns, toiletries, skincare, or any other aspect of their identity. I particularly dislike the limited gender options in Arabic, which only includes masculine and feminine pronouns. This lack of a neutral term is frustrating for those who don't identify as either male or female.

As a child, I felt like an outsider among family and relatives due to my unique personality. I knew I was different from everyone else. It was difficult to connect with others and build friendships, because I could not find people who shared my interests, ideas, and mindset.

In a country or city where being part of the LGBTQ+ community is not accepted you may face numerous challenges.

Since my facial hair started to grow, I have never been comfortable with it. So, I shave it frequently and pay close attention to my eyebrows. These actions have often led to conflicts with my family and society, but I have been determined to fight for the right to do what I like and express myself. I have been aware that this might come at a cost, but I believe it's important for people my age to challenge societal norms and explore their own identity.

Because of my focus on self-care and appearance, my parents labelled me 'effeminate.' Despite their disapproval, I continued to care for myself until my family issued several warnings and threats. They told me that if I did not stop, they would deny me money and restrict my freedom of movement, such as going out of the house after school. I was about 16 years old at the time.

My father was very religiously strict, but he did not have a strong presence at home, so he could not impose his opinions on me as forcefully as my mother did. He was largely absent from the family or social gatherings, spending most of his time engaged in religious rituals. He had little influence within the household. To intimidate me, my mother threatened to involve my uncle, a religiously and socially fanatic individual who is very concerned about the family's reputation. She told me: "If you don't cut your hair, I will make your uncle do whatever he likes to you."

My mother's concerns were how my feminine style or behaviour might damage the family's well-known reputation for religious commitment in the city and throughout the country. After much pressure to cut off my long hair, I eventually complied with her demand. However, I want to say that this decision was made based on my own values and circumstances at the time.

Social media became the only refuge I turned to for connection with people who share my interests, or at least accept me for who I am.

Given the global shortage of healthcare professionals, including nurses, I decided to pursue nursing studies. The news reports and social media discussions on this topic influenced my decision. I believe this field offers opportunities for relocation and the chance to contribute to a high-demand area. I graduated from the Faculty of Nursing with a strong academic record, but I'm currently working in a private company, in the customer service department. I do value my nursing degree, and this current role does not align with my career aspirations.

Most of my friends are online connections, either outside of Iraq or in other cities within the country. It's difficult to meet them in person. I do have a few friends in Najaf, but they are mostly lesbian girls who keep their identity hidden. Our friendships are mostly online. I'm also close to a drag queen artist, but their family restricts their movement, even if not knowing about their orientation. We mostly tried to meet at the university when possible.

My family can be intrusive, often calling me when I'm out, and limiting my ability to travel outside the city. I sometimes have had to lie to them, such as saying I was on a university trip so they would let me travel for a day or two.

I don't feel like I have a real family like others do. Living with them feels like being trapped in a prison. I'm forced to stay here, waiting for the day I can escape and live the life I want. Genetics are the only thing that connects me to my parents, but I did not choose to be their son. I have created my own personality separate from them. It sounds harsh, but I have to admit that I hate the house I live in and the outdated customs and traditions my parents have forced me to follow.

My identity is shaped by my own desires and self-education. As a queer person, I enjoy expressing myself through makeup and accessories. However, these acts are considered abnormal in my society and have led to threats and violence against me and others who do the same. Even my choice of clothing is seen as unconventional. I prefer feminine styles, which are often stigmatised by the male-dominated society. Living under these constraints, I long for the opportunity to leave Iraq and find a country that respects everyone, regardless of their religion, sexual orientation, or gender identity.

I remember one day I was wearing an earring, and someone who knew my family saw me and told my family about it. When my mother heard that I was wearing earrings, she phoned me while I was out and threatened to kill me, claiming that I was bringing 'shame' to the family. I was so scared. I took it off just to calm her down, but I still wear earrings in my room, just to please myself and do what I like.

I love accessories and have a large collection. At work, a client once asked me if I wore my earring for decoration or medical reasons. I found the question strange and intrusive, as it felt like a violation of my personal freedom.

My mother once accidentally discovered some female hormones injections in my room. She spent an hour lecturing me about how I was sick and needed a psychiatrist. She insisted on taking me to a doctor, but I refused. I'm not sick, I have just decided to be who I am.

In more recent years, I have carefully chosen my clothes and topics of conversation to avoid societal criticism. I often prioritise what society likes over my own preferences. This self-censorship makes it difficult to express myself authentically and freely. I'm always cautious about what I say and who I talk to, fearing that people might perceive me as LGBTQ+ and cause problems.

To protect myself from further threats, I changed my usernames, profile pictures, and posts on social media. I also made my accounts private to limit the access to my friends and people in my close circle.

The pressures I faced led me to a point where I started to hate my sexual orientation. No one understood me as a queer person, as I did not choose to be queer, and there was no one to support or accept me. However, connecting with other queer individuals on social media helped me overcome these difficulties. I have started to truly accept my identity and live with inner peace, at least. And then, I realised that the surrounding community is wrong, not me.

For LGBTQ+ content, I usually use X [previously Twitter] to post more freely than on other platforms. Every photo I post or text I write generates a large number of hateful comments, including incitements against me and calls for violence against LGBTQ+ people. My only crime is publishing content supporting my community, which I belong to and am proud to be part of.

These negative comments came from all parts of society, from students to police officers. Even those whose duty is supposed to protect individuals have been involved in intimidating and threatening LGBTQ+ people, including me, simply because we are different from societal stereotypes.

I received a disturbing threat on X. Someone commented on one of my posts, saying he wanted to know my address so that he could kill me. He also made derogatory remarks about my connection to the city of Najaf. I still have screenshots of these negative comments.

The constant fear and anxiety caused by haters have made me feel unsafe. When I go out, I'm constantly on edge, watching everyone around me for signs of danger. I once had a terrifying experience when someone had photographed me on the street and sent me photos on Instagram, threatening to harm me. After that, I was too afraid to leave my home for weeks, fearing kidnapping or worse.

It's clear these threats were intended to intimidate me and silence my online activism on LGBTQ+ issues. Their goal was to prevent me from sharing my experiences and advocating for equality.

I'm surrounded by threats, but it feels isolating to talk about them with my family. I'm worried they will just add to the pressure I am already feeling and keep me from living my life.

While in university, I faced bullying from my classmates. Even after graduating, they continued to spread rumours about me behind my back.

One day, a classmate told me that someone from the National Security

Agency had asked about me. I was so scared that I could not even stand up. A few days later, the University Student Affairs informed me that they were investigating my pro-LGBTQ+ posts on X. I was terrified that I would be expelled, lose my future opportunities, and be forced to stay at home.

The stress of the situation got worse when the University Legal Committee started questioning me. This happened on the day of an important exam, and I could not focus because I was so anxious and scared. The Committee had called me in for an interrogation right after the exam. They looked closely at my social media posts and asked if they were mine.

At first, I denied that the photos and posts were mine. But when they threatened legal action, I had to admit it. They documented what I said and made me sign a confession. A week later, I was suspended for a month.

The university ordeal did not end with my month-long dismissal. Later, I was shockingly informed that I had failed the entire year. This news devastated me, as it would have meant my family would find out and I would be delayed in achieving my goal of leaving Iraq. I pleaded with my teachers, breaking down emotionally. The Committee offered to reinstate me if I agreed to stop posting on social media, dress more conventionally, and change my appearance. I reluctantly complied, but this led to a period of depression that affected my self-care routine and overall well-being. For several months, I lost the desire to talk to people around me due to the shock I have experienced.

Since I was a student, and still now, I'm desperately searching for opportunities to escape home to a safer place. I contacted many of my feminist friends on X for help, and one activist suggested reaching out to IraQueer, an NGO that works with Iraqi LGBTQ+ individuals. Unfortunately, they could not help me leave the country. I know of many friends who have faced similar situations and tried to get help from IraQueer without success.

I'm hesitant to use gay dating apps due to the risk of infiltration by the state or militias. These apps can be dangerous for LGBTQ+ individuals in Iraq. I have heard of many people being targeted for using Grindr, a popular app in the country, as there are reports of unfriendly individuals embedded within the community to target LGBTQ+ individuals.

I thought about going to Lebanon or Turkey, countries that are known for being welcoming to LGBTQ+ people. Many people I know warned me against this plan, saying that it can take years to get asylum approval from the UN because there are so many applications. Also, I would need to find a way to support myself financially during this time, which would be difficult at first.

After trying everything else, I turned to international NGOs that are known for protecting LGBTQ+ individuals worldwide. I contacted Rainbow Railroad, an NGO that supports the community. However, most of these organisations required me to be outside of Iraq before they could help, which has been a major obstacle.

Despite working for a well-regarded company in Najaf, I find the workplace environment to be unsupportive of the LGBTQ+ community. Many of my colleagues hold traditional, masculine views, which can be challenging to navigate. To maintain my job and save up for my future plans, I have learned to adapt to their perspectives while being mindful of my own identity.

Hussein, 26, Basra

I'm Hussein, a 26-year-old gay man from Basra, the southernmost city in Iraq. I have lived here my whole life. When I was teenager, I realised I had feelings for guys. After the internet came to Iraq, I researched homosexuality and understood why I felt I'm different from others. Before that, I did not know what being gay meant.

I grew up in Karmat Ali district, not far from the city centre. My childhood was full of contradictions. From the outside, my life seemed normal. However, inside the house, the constant family problems between my father and mother caused me a lot of pain and suffering. I felt lonely and scared, and my ability to trust others was affected. Despite these challenges, I learned the importance of inner strength and resilience. I often had to rely on myself to manage my daily affairs at home.

I'm the second child in my family. When my father was imprisoned during the time of former president Saddam Hussein (before 2003), my mother was pregnant with me. After his release, my father longed for my older brother, who is one year older than me. The focus of attention was on my older brother until the birth of my younger brother, who is four years younger than me. At that point, the attention shifted from my older brother to the youngest. I did not understand why this was happening and never asked my parents about it. I felt like an outsider in my own family, for reasons I couldn't understand.

The family problems persisted for many years. I often envied my relatives, who had stable lives with regular routines. Their lunchtime and bedtime were always consistent, something that was missing from our home due to the problems. I wished I had been born into a stable family and could enjoy a peaceful life.

When I was 14, we moved to Al-Haritha, a neighbourhood in another part of the city. This area has a strong tribal and religious character. Moving here was a shock for me and somewhat unsettling. As a result, I spent most of my time at home. After my parents divorced in 2019, things became more peaceful. My older brother got married, and his wife was very kind to us. Unfortunately, my father passed away from COVID-19. My older brother, his wife, and I moved in to care for the house, while my mother went to live with her brother.

Some neighbours do not even know I belong to the family because they have not seen me outside. I prefer to avoid socialising with the community. This society does not understand me or respect my sexual orientation as a gay man. This forces me to hide who I am from everyone.

Looking back on my childhood, I cannot recall many specific details. The school I attended with my cousins was quite far from home. I had to walk there, which was difficult, but I could not afford a private taxi like others. As time went on, my cousins dropped out of school, leaving me as the only one attending. I even took a year off at one point, but eventually decided to return when my brother and a cousin enrolled the school again. Although I continued to go, the presence of some unruly students made me prefer to head straight home after school.

The boys on my street used to play football. Unfortunately, I was not very good at the game, which made me feel excluded from their teams. As a result, I started playing with my young female cousins. Some people made negative comments about me playing with girls, especially in my tribal community where it was seen as shameful for boys to play with girls. Despite the criticism, I enjoyed playing with them and even helped them in the kitchen. I also began to enjoy playing pretend kitchen games. However, the negative comments continued, even coming from my family, who disapproved of my preference for playing with girls instead of boys.

When I was 12, I had sex with one of my relatives who is a year older than me, a male cousin who enjoyed having sex with boys. One day, he told me to come over and have sex with him when no one else would be home, so we went and had sex. We actually had sex without intercourse, and it scared me and surprised me because it was the first time I had sex.

When I was 14, I developed a crush on a handsome classmate. While other students often misbehaved, he was always calm and gentle, which drew me to him. Over time, my feelings for him grew stronger. His house was close to mine, making it easy for us to see each other frequently. Later, I discovered that my mother knew his mother, which strengthened our connection and made it more convenient for us to visit each other. Perhaps because of my young age or the conservative nature of my tribal community, I was hesitant to express my feelings openly. I feared the consequences of doing so, even though my love for this classmate was genuine. I didn't tell him about my feelings, and our relationship did not last long due to me moving to a new area at that age.

In my new school I met someone who caught my eye on the first day. His name was Hassan, and his unique style of clothes stood out from the others, attracting me to him. While he was not as handsome as the first person I was interested in, I liked his appearance. He was also tall, which was another quality I admired in a person. We made eye contact in the schoolyard, and then I left. Next day, my father and I went to a nearby farm to buy vegetables. As we stood by the tomatoes, I saw Hassan near the farm. He looked at me, smiled, laughed, and pointed at me. My father and I bought our tomatoes and went home.

Hassan and I were in a long-term relationship that continued until the first year of university. At the beginning of our relationship, we enjoyed a peaceful connection without physical intimacy. Although I desired it, he refused due to his religious beliefs and internal conflict. As he matured, he began to reject the relationship, stating that our actions were *haram* and displeasing to God. I recall only one instance when he removed his shirt in front of me, revealing a glimpse of his physique. We eventually parted ways due to his internal conflict between accepting his homosexuality and adhering to the societal customs, traditions, and religious restrictions imposed by Islam. His religious commitment made it difficult for him to reconcile these two aspects of his life.

My subsequent relationships were brief and fleeting. I became more cautious about meeting and forming connections with others due to the challenges of being a homosexual in a conservative religious area. I have always been mindful of my online interactions and behaviour, as public displays of affection or sexual orientation could lead to serious consequences, including social ostracism, potential violence, or even death. In my society, being gay is considered a disgrace to one's family and clan, and I fear the unknown fate that could befall me if my sexual orientation were to become public knowledge.

I initially loved the Arabic language, but found the academic experience at the University of Basra less fulfilling than expected. Having completed one year of language studies, I switched to port studies. After graduating in 2021, I struggled to find employment in my field. I had hoped that studying there would lead to quicker job prospects. Unfortunately, circumstances forced me to find work in various fields to support myself. I have always been passionate about farming and worked on a farm for a time. I also worked for an interior decoration company, and now I'm a secretary in a doctor's office. While this is not my dream job, it at least helps me cover my living expenses.

Outside of work hours, I do not have a strict daily routine. I spend my time doing chores like cooking, washing clothes, and taking care of the garden. Sometimes, I simply relax and do nothing. My love for cooking probably developed out of necessity. Growing up, I had to take care of myself due to the family problems. My mother was not always able to cook, so I learned to do it myself. Over time, I became quite good at it. As for my hobbies, I enjoy drawing anime and strange characters. I also love reading poetry collections in classical Arabic.

Facebook was the first platform I used to connect with the LGBTQ+ community in Iraq. I created a fake account to protect my privacy and avoid potential harm from family or friends. I was curious about the discussions in Facebook groups. Some members shared personal stories and experiences related to their bodies, relationships, and sexuality. I found these discussions interesting and learned more about being LGBTQ+. Through Facebook groups I have met people and formed friendships within the community. It has been a valuable resource for connection and support.

After some time, I decided to leave Facebook for a while, and in 2019 switched to using Grindr to connect with other gay people. However, I did not find the app to be entirely trustworthy. Many users provide deceitful information, and there's always the risk of hacking and online harassment. So, I used the app cautiously, browsing profiles briefly and then leaving. I did not spend much time actively engaging with others.

I struggled to find a lasting relationship. I met someone on Facebook, and we started talking. We felt a connection and played PUBG together. During the game, he expressed romantic feelings, which I reciprocated. We communicated online for a while and eventually decided to meet and have soft sex. His house was near the University of Basra, which was convenient for me.

After having had casual soft sex several times, we decided to have full sexual intercourse. I went to his place, and it was my first experience with intense sexual activity. This happened in 2020, and around the same time my relationship with Hassan had ended. Hassan told me he wanted to marry a woman, which was a shock, but I respectfully accepted his decision. I tried to move on by focusing on other relationships. Anyway, I had an open relationship with this new person. We both agreed to have sex with whoever we wanted without restrictions. But once I told him about having sex with someone else, he became upset. I sensed he was starting to develop feelings for me and wanted our relationship to be more exclusive.

After my father passed away from COVID-19, we continued our sexual encounters about once a week. However, I started experiencing symptoms and discovered I had an HPV infection. My weakened immune system made me susceptible to the infection, which I believe was transmitted from him due to his unprotected sexual activity. To protect my health, I ended the relationship and avoided further contact to prevent serious complications. Since 2020, we have not seen each other.

In Iraqi society, it's customary for men to marry in order of age, especially in rural or tribal areas. This can be frustrating for me as a gay man, as I'm often questioned and criticised about my relationship status. People frequently ask why I have not married yet. To avoid further inquiries, I usually respond by saying that I'm not ready and want to focus on my career. This helps me deflect their curiosity and avoid unnecessary scrutiny.

I feel unsafe in Iraq, especially since the government enacted laws criminalising same-sex relationships in 2024. These laws restrict freedoms and threaten my safety. I have become more cautious about interacting with others, only meeting people I trust.

Like many young Iraqis, I considered emigrating years ago to find a better life. However, financial constraints as a student prevented me from pursuing that option. As living in Basra has its challenges due to my sexual orientation, I try to navigate my life discreetly.

Bash Taha, 34, Berlin

I'm Bash Taha, an Iraqi Kurdish gay man, born in Baghdad in 1990 into a wealthy and educated family. Although born in the capital, I essentially grew up in Iraqi Kurdistan. My early years were marked by a lack of stability, shaped by a variety of challenges, especially due to my homosexuality and effeminate appearance, which did not fit in with the societal norms.

My childhood memories are centred around our home on Palestine Street in downtown Baghdad, and my school life. Despite my family's considerable wealth from my father's successful business, my parents were always cautious about my feminine appearance and behaviour and limited my interactions with the outside world.

My mother worked as a university lecturer and was busy teaching for most of the day. She was extremely concerned about people finding out that her son is gay. She believed it would bring shame upon her and the entire family due to our family's close ties to those in power. There was also the worry that people might blame her for promoting homosexuality among her students, simply because her son is gay or had a slightly different appearance.

I often felt neglected as my parents were so preoccupied with their demanding jobs. I yearned for their attention and support, but their hectic schedules left me feeling deprived. I recall a rare moment when my father pulled me onto his lap, providing a fleeting sense of warmth amidst his work and travels. My mother, with her passion for teaching, travel, and other interests, often seemed emotionally distant. I found comfort in the company of the nanny, as I spent more time with her than with my parents.

Despite having a few friends from school, my parents rarely permitted me to socialise outside of the classroom. It was discouraging not being able to play with my friends after school, but I had no option but to comply with their rules. It was a rather lonely childhood. I remember our private chauffeur driving me to and from school daily, while the nanny, whose native language was English, became a major influence in my life, inspiring me to develop a love for English over Arabic.

However, my friends have always been extremely supportive and understanding, like a second family. I could open up to them about everything in my life, sharing my thoughts and feelings without hesitation. They were my safe space, accepting me for who I truly am. Instead of judging or teasing, they encouraged me to be proud of myself, which was exactly what I needed. I did not know what LGBTQ+ meant, but I always felt like I was a special boy compared to others.

Chaos started in my life when I was eleven. My family made the choice to relocate us from Baghdad to Dohuk in Iraqi Kurdistan to escape the constant negativity that surrounded me. However, this decision brought about a whole new set of unexpected events. My parents and I used to go on short trips to visit our relatives in Kurdistan. But this time they, unexpectedly, left me with my relatives and returned to Baghdad, leaving my future uncertain. They seemed to have vanished out of thin air. The memory of their vow to come back again from Baghdad have stayed with me as the last image I have of them fading away from my life.

Adapting to life in Dohuk was a significant challenge. My upbringing in Baghdad was not heavily influenced by religion; instead, it was characterised by unique experiences. For instance, red wine was a common presence at our dinner table, symbolising a sense of freedom for my parents. However, I continued to keep my sexual orientation to myself until I reached a more mature age.

When I entered my teenage years, still living with my cousins' family, I was constantly bombarded with negative comments about my appearance and behaviour from both neighbours and relatives. The family I lived in also faced scrutiny from others, who criticised my long hair, eyelashes, and perceived femininity. I was even given the nickname 'Bashira,' a popular female name in Iraq, which further fuelled the disapproval I faced from society. People often blamed my parents for not having raised me in a more traditional Iraqi way, which led to feelings of self-doubt and negativity within me.

While they never directly addressed the issue, it was clear that my cousins' family was uncomfortable with any public displays of my identity or appearance. Their primary concern seemed to be how my more flamboyant characteristics might affect our family's reputation. In their view, as well as in the eyes of society, I was challenging traditional norms.

My older relatives tended to disapprovingly recognise me for being authentic to who I really am, but my passion for art made some of them more accepting. My aunt always showered me and my younger cousins with gifts, picking out special presents and stylish clothes. I remember one time she surprised me with a red T-shirt, while my cousins received more typical boys' toys like water guns.

It's been a while since I lost all my childhood memories because of the distance I have felt for so long. My parents' faces have become blurry in my mind; I would not recognise them if I passed them on the street. Maybe they keep tabs on me through social media, like silent spectators, but I do not have any connection with them or any of my relatives. As far as I know, they are now living in the UAE, close in proximity but far away emotionally. Even though I might bump into them some day, I'm not actively seeking them out.

I often found myself questioning why certain things happened to me instead of others. What could possibly be the cause of the discrimination I faced? Was it based on my emotions or my appearance? These questions haunted me, leaving a deep emotional scar.

During my adolescence, I discovered a profound sense of comfort in the music of Michael Jackson, which resonated with me on a significant level. His songs of love, acceptance, and self-expression became the soundtrack of my life, providing reassurance that I was not alone in my struggles. In spite of the criticism and scrutiny I faced from people, I remained steadfast in my conviction that authenticity was paramount, far outweighing the pressure to conform to societal expectations. I can say that Jackson's music served as a beacon of inspiration, encouraging me to celebrate my uniqueness and to remain resilient in the face of challenges.

However, the world did not always have the sound of Michael Jackson's music or the support of my friends. There existed a darkness as well. One time, while walking down the street when I was still living with my parents in Baghdad, I was the victim of sexual harassment. I was left feeling shaken and scared by the violation. When I hurried back home, hoping for comfort in my mother's embrace, the impact I felt was even more profound. She heard me out, but her words were filled with shame instead of solace. "Your name is in everyone's mouth," she said, her tone weighted: "The word is that you are gay, and it reflects poorly on our family."

In my teenage years, something really confusing happened in the company of my cousins, who were my age and older. We were hanging out and they suggested we check out some porn. The video started off with straight stuff, and while they seemed to be enjoying it, I found myself more drawn to the guy, imagining what it would be like to be with him. My cousins picked up on something being different about me, maybe in how I was acting or looking. We were all pretty teenagers, and our families definitely did not talk about stuff like that back then.

I lived with my cousins in Dohuk for several years, where I developed feelings for one of my older cousins. Initially, our bond was based on friendship and support, but it eventually evolved into a romantic relationship. During times of loneliness and sadness, he offered comfort by holding me close, and our love was expressed through physical affection and kisses, all while keeping it hidden from the rest of his family. In 2013, we shared an intimate sexual moment for the first time, and despite feeling a bit apprehensive, I felt safe with him. He was more than just my love; he was close family.

In my early twenties, I decided to chase after my dream of becoming an artist. I was inspired by the beauty of painting, photography, and makeup, especially when it came to capturing the essence of women. I longed for my artistic talents to be acknowledged. But fate had led me to Kurdistan, a place where being gay was not that great, although at least better than in other Iraqi cities. Furthermore, learning the Kurdish language was a challenge, but my passion for art never faltered.

After graduating from high school in Dohuk, I enrolled in the acting diploma course at the Institute of Fine Arts. Due to the distance from my cousins' house, I alternated between staying with them and living in the institute's dorms. Despite the challenges of balancing my studies, personal life, and relationships, I successfully completed the course with excellent grades. Following graduation, I secured a receptionist position at a city-based TV station. Nonetheless, it was a good starting point, even though the salary was low at just over $200.

While working at the local television station. I closely observed the styling of the news anchors and presenters. One lucky day, when the makeup artist fell ill, a presenter asked me to do her makeup right then and there! To my surprise, everyone, including the manager, was impressed. They recognised my skills and promoted me from receptionist to makeup artist! In Dohuk, my distinctive makeup skills quickly set me apart. As a young man, I became known for my ability to enhance women's beauty. This talent caught the eye of one of the local TV station directors, who offered me the chance to host my own makeup show, 'Bashar Style.' The show featured my makeup techniques and offered beauty advice to viewers and the women I had as guests.

'Bashar Style' became a hit, proving that men can successfully host shows about women's beauty. My passion for the industry and unique style led to a new opportunity in Erbil, where I could continue my work and expand my reputation. My success in Erbil led to a rewarding career and a lavish lifestyle. But despite initial promises of safety, my growing popularity in Erbil led to unwanted advances from politicians at private gatherings or parties. I politely declined their inappropriate requests for sexual favours.

I can say that my life and time in Kurdistan was a true challenge. Despite the years that went by and the impact they had on me; my destiny remained uncertain. I longed for a fresh start; a life brimming with possibilities.

Throughout this time, my boyfriend supported me in every step, stood by my side, and encouraged me to continue my journey of success and pursue the work I love and dream of. However, his family had a strict tradition of marrying off their sons in a specific order, starting with the oldest. As the second son, he was expected to marry next. Despite my strong feelings for him, my fear led me to act impulsively. I tried to convince him not to get married, even though I understood the importance of this tradition to his family.

The situation was even more complex because he was bisexual. In retrospect, I realise that his frequent weekend visits to my house might have raised suspicions, especially since he was not following his family's expectations regarding marriage. It all ended in 2014. His family became suspicious and curious about our relationship and the time we spent together. Out of nowhere, his dad barged in on us at my house, finding us in bed. We were watching a movie and eating popcorn in bed at my house in the Italian Village of Erbil when I noticed a shadow entering the doorway. I questioned whether someone had entered the house. "Don't worry," my partner assured me. But our reassurance was shattered when his father stormed in, finding us both undressed. He struck me violently with the butt of his gun, causing me to bleed heavily from my head. He then left the scene, abandoning his son and me. I have not heard from him since, and my relationship with my partner ended.

A few days later, I departed from Kurdistan and stayed in Turkey for a time. Then, I attempted an illegal sea crossing to Europe.

I endured a harrowing migration journey, making three unsuccessful attempts to reach Europe via Turkey. Each time, I was apprehended at the Turkish border and deported. Finally, I managed to cross with the help of four smugglers from Afghanistan and other countries, after paying hundreds and hundreds of dollars.

I cannot adequately describe the horrors I experienced during my hard journey from Turkey to Europe. Travelling through treacherous seas, mountains, and forests, I faced unimaginable cruelty when the smugglers repeatedly forced me to have sex, leaving me no choice but to comply or else risk my life.

Every time they demanded sex, I was forced to comply, even though I wept in protest. They persisted with their demands throughout the entire, arduous journey. I pleaded with them to stop, but their abuse only intensified. They took advantage of my vulnerability, relentlessly subjecting me to their torment. I endured days on the road, covered in their sperms, unable to wash my body.

The day I arrived in Germany, I felt a sense of relief and safety, finally finding a place I could call home. Learning a new language and adapting to a different culture allowed me to showcase my abilities.

Berlin just felt like the perfect place for me to settle down. It was, and still is, like my safe haven, welcoming me with warmth and acceptance. Back in Iraq, life was tough due to prejudice and discrimination. But here in Berlin, I can finally be myself without any fear. No more feeling like an outsider or being judged unfairly.

Being in a safe place where I can live my life freely, chase my dream career, and finally enjoy the freedoms I missed out on feels amazing. I used to just watch Pride Month celebrations on social media, but now I get to be a part of it all.

My dreams really came true the moment I arrived in Europe. Here I am, Bash, feeling so lucky!

Azad Issa, 37, London

My name is Azad Issa, I'm a gay man from Dohuk, Iraqi Kurdistan. Born in 1987, I lived there until late 2023. Seeking safety and acceptance away from my family and society, I moved to the capital. Unfortunately, I discovered that Baghdad, like many places, is not a safe haven for LGBTQ+ individuals.

Despite my lifelong dream of becoming an actor, the underdeveloped arts sector in my hometown, Dohuk, forced me to prioritise finding work to survive. The constant struggle to make ends meet has left little time for pursuing my artistic passions. However, I'm determined to find ways to combine my work with my creative aspirations, whether it's through exploring opportunities within my current field or connecting with other artists online.

Despite these challenges, I remained hopeful that one day I will achieve my dreams. But first, I needed to find a safe place where I can freely express my creativity and identity as a gay man without facing challenges or obstacles.

At fourteen, I realised I was attracted to boys. Back then, I had no one to confide in and didn't fully understand what I was going through. Being gay was, and still is, a taboo subject in my society. The fear of societal and familial backlash made me hesitant to come out.

As I got older, the pressure to conform to societal expectations became overwhelming. I felt like I had to hide my true self from everyone. Living in a small city like Dohuk, where everyone knows each other, made it even riskier to be openly gay. To stay safe, I presented myself as straight. My masculine appearance helped me hide who I am and the feelings inside.

In Dohuk, a city where people follow old traditions, it was hard for me to live as a gay man. People would question why I was not married yet. The constant fear of judgment made me cautious about meeting new people and discussing my true feelings. I was always afraid that people would find out and hurt me. Even when I moved to Baghdad, things did not get better. It was very difficult to pretend to be someone else, but I had to do it to stay safe.

I'm always careful about what I wear to avoid getting bad comments. I consider myself lucky that my masculine look often keeps people from guessing I'm gay. Despite adapting to hiding my inclinations from people, it remained emotionally draining for me, as I was living a way I didn't want or desire, where I didn't feel like I was expressing my true self.

As part of the LGBTQ+ community, we often face societal pressures to conform to traditional norms. This is a daily struggle for me. Even though I have a masculine appearance, which can offer some protection, being gay still presents challenges. Those who are more visibly gay, through their appearance or mannerisms, may face greater risks. My masculine presentation has helped me keep my sexual orientation hidden for a long time.

I have succeeded to some extent in hiding my orientation from others, but this matter had negative psychological consequences, as I feel lonely due to my inability to always share my true identity with others. I also suffer a lot from constant anxiety, stress, and discomfort because I'm unable to show what's inside me in public.

In Dohuk, being part of the LGBTQ+ community was incredibly challenging. Our community is often divided based on how masculine or feminine we appear. Sadly, people in my society associate being gay with feminine traits, which leads to discrimination and violence against those who fit that stereotype.

The deeply religious background of Iraqi society, combined with laws that criminalise same-sex sexual acts, contributes to the prejudice and discrimination faced by us, the LGBTQ+ community. This puts us at risk of arrest, imprisonment, or other forms of harm.

Like countless others, I desperately yearned to escape the harsh realities of my homeland and find a place where I can truly be myself. Despite my efforts to seek assistance from international NGOs, I faced significant obstacles. These organisations often have narrow and stereotypical views of what it means to be gay, focusing solely on outward appearances rather than the individual's identity. This has led to a frustrating and disheartening experience for me and many others like me.

Let me tell you about an incident that happened to me while chatting with someone on Grindr. I got to know someone who worked for the United Nations in Iraq. Through this person, I tried to seek advice and help to enable me to leave the country. However, when he saw the photos I shared with him, he told me that my masculine appearance would not qualify me to convince international organisations of my orientation, or even have my file accepted at all. This caused me great disappointment. Since that incident, I no longer tried to seek asylum from international organisations concerned with protecting human rights and organising protective asylum applications. Driven to desperation, I could have to resort to dangerous and illegal means to reach Europe, risking my life in perilous journeys fraught with human trafficking. However, with limited options and no legal path to my dream destination, I felt trapped. All I desired was a place where I can feel safe, accepted, and free to express my true self.

My dream of finding a lifelong partner had become my ultimate desire, a dream that I find increasingly difficult to realise in Iraq. I attribute this difficulty to several factors, including societal pressures against any individuals living together without familial ties, the immaturity I perceived in a significant portion of the LGBTQ+ community in Iraq, and the reduction of homosexuality to mere sexual acts, a common misconception in the Middle East. These obstacles, I believe, hindered my ability to find a partner who shares my values and aspirations.

Even if I were to find the person I have been seeking for years, the idea of living together in Iraq seems like nothing more than a wishful dream. I would be putting myself at risk of threats, hatred, incitement, and violence, which could ultimately lead to my death. Expressing one's sexual orientation in Iraq can be extremely dangerous. It's like social, if not physical, suicide.

As an LGBTQ+ individual living in Iraq, I faced constant threats to my life. After receiving numerous death threats, I was forced to flee the country illegally in July 2024. Due to Iraq's harsh new laws criminalising homosexuality, which carry a potential 15-year prison sentence, I couldn't report the threats to the authorities. Tragically, many LGBTQ+ individuals have perished in Iraqi prisons, including 'Jojo,' a transgender person whose death I believe was linked to prison authorities. With no legal way to escape, and fearing for my life, I had no choice but to begin a risky journey through Turkey to seek safety outside its border.

During my refugee journey from Turkey to Britain, I endured immense suffering and hardship. I do not want to delve into the details as I'm still grappling with the psychological effects. From the moment I left Turkey until I arrived in Britain, I experienced fear, anxiety, hunger, beatings, humiliation, and exhaustion.

I left everything behind—my job, my apartment, my car—in search of safety and freedom abroad. But the journey was far from easy. In Bulgaria, I faced a major crisis when the authorities arrested me. Despite breaking the law by entering illegally, the reality of prison was crushing. At 37 years of age, I found myself crying like a baby, asking, 'Why am I here?' I had escaped death in Iraq, only to end up imprisoned and beaten. For three days, I could not even walk.

After my release from Bulgarian prison, I continued my arduous journey across Europe, finally reaching France. I lived in the forests of France before making my way to Britain. The weeks it took to reach Britain were filled with unimaginable suffering, and I'm desperate to forget those memories. Now, I'm getting help from a psychologist to heal from the trauma of my refugee journey. Every time I recount my experiences, I'm overwhelmed by anxiety and tears.

In the forests of France, international NGOs would come to us, bringing food and clothes. Yet, at the end of the day, I found myself sleeping in the middle of the forest, uncertain about the future. The harsh conditions I endured have left such a deep mark that, even after reaching Britain and being provided with hotel accommodation by the British government, I was waking up every night for two weeks, haunted by visions of myself still lost in the French forests.

I reached out to several LGBTQ+ organisations in Britain, hoping for psychological support, recognition of my sexual orientation, and documentation to strengthen my asylum case. Unfortunately, many of them were unable to provide the assistance I needed. Then I asked, 'What is the purpose of these organisations if they cannot offer such crucial support?' Imagine arriving in a new country with nothing but a damaged phone and a meagre 20 euros.

I contacted the National Health Service (NHS) to help me find a psychologist who could help me overcome the anxiety and obsession I'm suffering from, which even affects my speech. I had two asylum interviews, and in each one, I cried while speaking, felt short of breath, and could not continue the conversation. I'm suffering a lot because of what happened to me.

Here in Britain, within the shared accommodation where I live, which is occupied by immigrants from various countries, most people do not accept the concept of homosexuality. Once, I discussed homosexuality with my roommate, but he expressed his disapproval and refused to talk about it. However, outside of the place, there is a great deal of freedom for me to live and experience the life I want and desire. I feel more liberated in terms of gender identity and freedom of clothing without the restrictions I had in Iraq. But I'm anticipating an uncertain future. I do not know if my asylum application will be accepted or rejected, and I might be deported back to Iraq, which is something I dread.

If I were to return to Iraq, I would be killed due to the threats I received shortly before leaving Iraq. I fled without saying goodbye to my family. I only told them after I left the country. Everyone was shocked by my decision to flee. They all asked why. Because everyone knows I have a job and a stable career. But I cannot tell my family and friends that I left because of my sexual orientation and the threats I received.

I chose to come to Britain because it's the right place for me. It's a suitable environment for gay people, where I can express myself freely, wear the clothes I want—and my rights are protected. Beyond my sexual orientation, I'm simply a human being. I yearn for a life free from discrimination and prejudice. All I seek is the right to live.

About the author

Azhar Al-Rubaie was born in 1992 in Basra, a city in southern Iraq known for its rich history and cultural heritage. He is an Iraqi journalist, researcher, and writer whose work spans pan-Arab and international media outlets, including the BBC, The Telegraph, Al Jazeera, Middle East Eye, VICE, The Arab Weekly, The New Arab, Raseef22, and many others. Since 2019, he works as a correspondent for Deutsche Welle Arabic in Iraq.

Al-Rubaie's firsthand accounts of significant events, such as the Basra uprising and the 2019 mass protests, have captured the essence of these pivotal moments in Iraqi history. Known for his analytical pieces, he has collaborated with The Washington Institute for Near East Policy and has worked as an assistant researcher in the fields of water, environment, and climate change with the London School of Economics.

Al-Rubaie began his journalism career in 2014. His reporting covers a wide range of critical issues, including post-ISIS events, national protests, politics and corruption, water scarcity, environmental and climate change challenges, and human rights. In addition to his journalistic work, he has collaborated with the Aliph Foundation to document and support the preservation of Iraq's cultural heritage in cities such as Baghdad, Mosul, and Dohuk.

www.ingramcontent.com/pod-product-compliance
Lightning Source LLC
LaVergne TN
LVHW061601070526
838199LV00077B/7132